→ GOOD GIRL

→ FOR JODY STEWART

who has repeatedly lent me her intelligence to hold on to
as I've waded through the quicksand of my Wynne, Arkansas mind.

ACKNOWLEDGMENTS

Earlier versions of these poems have been published in the following magazines or journals:

Art/Life: "Safari Through the South"; "The Muses Have Moved In"; "Being Terrific"; "Last Phase of the Moon"

Barrow Street: "The Cuckoo Doesn't Know When to Come Out"

DayBreak: "The Vessel Won't Hold Water"; "Pyramids, Rome, and Pharaohs"; "The Design of Random"

rivertalk: "Introduction"; "Beginning"; "Bruised Waters"; "What Hester Prynne Told Young Women Who Came to Her as an Expert on Trouble"; "Postcard: The Geography of Mailboxes"; "Working My Way Up"; "No One Has Asked for My Word on Things"; "Answering Back"; "The Romance of Civil War"; "Arrival"; "Outside Barstow"; "The Visit"; "Running Loose Around the Castle"

Solo: "Mirror on the Wall"; "Talking to Elena"

Verve: "Larger Than I Am"; "The Woman Who Wears Black Most Days"

"Conrad's Mother" and "Introduction" appeared in *Beyond the Valley of Contemporary Poets Anthology*, 1997.

I am especially grateful to Alane Rollings for her subtle, deft editorial skills. She gave unstintingly of her time and sensibilities to this manuscript. I can't ever thank her enough for her generosity.

The quotations that appear in this book are used by permission of the following publishers:

Copyright © 1998 by Tim Parks. Reprinted from *Adultery and Other Diversions* by Tim Parks, published by Arcade Publishing, New York, New York.

Copyright © 1976 by Samuel Beckett. Reprinted from *A Samuel Beckett Reader* edited by Richard W. Seaver, published by Grove/Atlantic, Inc., New York, New York.

Contents

→ GARMENT DISTRICT

5   Outside Barstow

8   The Romance of Civil War

9   Mirror on the Wall

11   Running Loose Around the Castle

12   The Design of Random

→ HAIRDRESSER

17   Conrad's Mother

19   Pyramids, Rome, and Pharaohs

21   Introduction

23   Working My Way Up

24   Was Eden a Gated Community?

→ TANNING BOOTH

29   The Woman Who Wears Black Most Days

30   Books

32   Books II

33   Postcard: The Geography of Mailboxes

34   Gather at the River

36   Sitting in a Room

37   No One Has Asked for My Word on Things

39   Garlands

→ MANICURIST

43   Beginning

44   Speaking to My Granddaughter

48 Talking to Elena

50 Reading at the Tujunga Library

→ PLASTIC SURGEON

55 Geology of Home

59 Larger than I Am

61 The Visit

62 Wife of Polonius

65 Answering Back

→ ETIQUETTE BOOK

69 Taking Conspicuous Consumption on the Road

71 Real Estate

73 Talking to People You Can't See

75 What Hester Prynne Told Young Women Who Came to Her as an Expert on Trouble

77 Bruised Waters

→ COSMETICS IN THE PURSE

81 The Cuckoo Doesn't Know When to Come Out

84 The Muses Have Moved In

86 Being Terrific

87 Last Phase of the Moon

89 Bruised Waters II

92 Arrival

→ HAG HOUSE

95 The Vessel Won't Hold Water

96 Mother of Jonah

98 The Journey: What We Take with Us

101 Aria from This Opera Called My Life

105 Safari Through the South

➔GOOD GIRL

✦ GARMENT DISTRICT

"...the Olympians were hardly fair in obliterating people who could not see that a beggar was a god."

TIM PARKS

Outside Barstow

I

The Swan Song Cafe is full of late-night truckers,
Las Vegas types and strays, but only one waitress.
She's overweight. You can almost hear her feet hurting,

pressing against her shoes like parents making love
in a quiet house. Asleep in the car, my twenty-year-old son
is no more help than when he was four. We traveled

cross-country that year, too. He slept in the front seat
on top of the tomato soup box filled with books,
a nice fit. We had a lot in common then –

a destiny of hot roast beef sandwiches, iced tea,
bacon and eggs, strong coffee, and stained silverware.
They roll across the countertop now as if they, too,

have come 4,000 miles. The seams of the waitress's girdle
show under the nylon of her dress. Roads she took for
one reason or another. She's nice to me. I'm grateful.

Vulnerable in the fluorescent light, bone-marrow tired,
I'm too old to do with any style what I'm doing. Two months
of the summer gouged out, I'm reaching for home.

Emptiness is ahead. I keep moving, anyway.
The black hole of my past sucks at my heels.
I look behind me only when sitting at counters

after midnight in places like Barstow: the Wicked
Sorcerer, the Queen of Swans. Ponds of light
along American highways disappear at dawn.

II

In the car, my arms and legs stick out as if they belong
to a stuffed bear propped on a bed. There are worse spells
than Von Rotbart's. The steering wheel, the accelerator,

the brakes, the clutch disguise what causes this posture.
The arms and legs will do almost anything
but the rest of the body knows better.

There's no place on earth except where
you are. There is no home,
only the lake that the heart makes.

III

The town where I've lived for years turns out
to be uglier than Fillmore, Kentucky;
Bucksnort, Tennessee; Gallup, New Mexico.

The carpet in my apartment could camouflage rattlesnakes.
It all looks unhealthy, shabby, cramped. I try to imagine how
hard I must have worked to keep facts from killing me.

In my bedroom upstairs, I light candles
late at night. It takes the truth
small flames tell to ease me into sleep.

IV

Thomas played with the tresses of a homeward angel.
Others have shaved its head.
Mark of the raped woman. Bald eagle of a nation

in high-rent, low-cost housing. Low-limbed nest
with just enough windows to see
the heart beat itself to death against a blue sky.

The Romance of Civil War

The man in the brown plaid jacket and bowler hat
is the one who interests me. You can have
all those Confederate stone walls, genuflecting
captains, drum and bugle boys who've volunteered
their way into the greenest of fields. Keep them
right there in Perryville, Kentucky, re-enacting
themselves until snow or rain makes them go home.
A rifle shoots true if anyone
who knows how to aim enters the ranks.

They do this poppycock thing out at Fort Tejon
along Interstate 5 spring and fall. I think they
ought to do it in the dead of winter without flu
shots. Wars are always fought in the dead of
winter. Any rusted toy tin soldier can tell you that.

I'm driving along, come upon a woman stranded
on the freeway. I start to stop but see she is
a Yuppie with a cellular phone. Her blonde
skirt and silk hair swirl in the wind. She has
her back turned to the platoon of Confederate
soldiers marching two abreast over a green knoll
parallel the road. I wonder if they will help her,
if she will know who they are when she turns
around to meet the wind. I must remember never
to break down anywhere near Fort Tejon.

Mirror on the Wall

I've lived in Memphis, Chicago, Laramie, Knoxville,
San Francisco, Pidgeon Forge, Palo Alto
yet never looked as if I were from anywhere.
The taint of a hick still hangs on my shoulders like a shawl,

a flimsy gypsy's thing, not the thick wool cape a good Irish
Catholic woman would pull over her head.
People have taken to introducing me as the woman
who's come all the way from Bakersfield...

a public novelty, a first sighting.
My levis suggest hardship —
as if one can travel from Bakersfield only by horse.
Going out the door today, needing to be in Santa Barbara by sunset,

I catch a glimpse of myself in the mirror.
I distinctly look as if I belong where I am.
The image surprises me. I never thought I'd end up
playing a supporting role in a *National Geographic* documentary.

Living in Bakersfield is like any other thing:
alcohol, drugs, gambling, passion.
Once you've done it, it's hard not to go on doing it.
Even a weekend away and you begin to look strung out.

Drinking tea in Fillmore, I hear California's jokes about Bakersfield.
"It isn't the end of the world, but the edge can be seen from there."
Stunning as a lead sinker, Fillmore would be the place
to tell the wide-open truth to the chosen few passing through.

II

Once, the beloved daughter.
There's no sup of holy water on the dresser.
Once, a woman.
She disappeared in a tangle of sheets.
Once, a mother.
My son's daughter stares at me as she would any stranger.

Without the foliage of love, you and I are raw earth.
Our eyes are lost maps that pirates drew.
The hard, dark Edge is but part of the X on a larger map
older than any bouquet of cities
God delivers to your door.

Running Loose Around the Castle

The grass skirt on the willow is yellow this morning.
Just above a shallow pool,
the long, flowing skirt of Ophelia sways in the wind,

pale yellow the right color for a young girl.
She's poor enough now her daddy's dead.
Shining through the tattered skirt is the flesh of sunlight.

Her mind having snapped sometime ago,
she recites the limericks of herbs. Legs,
paler than even these leaves, twirl on feet

I cannot possibly see from this window
although I'm sure she's out there
barefoot in December.

The Design of Random

She sits in the afternoon, watching sunlight press against the floor,
her purse on the wicker stool nearby.
She studies the elongated shadow of the stool, its legs
those of a crane half submerged in a pool of sunlight.
But then wicker curls the way wicker always does.

A circle of darkness contains three bright spots.
Eventually, these canapés of light are taken up,
eaten by time as if it had a mouth and appetite,
the dark plate left empty.

Her bare feet are cold, the patio door open behind her.
In spite of the sweet lies of sunlight, air keeps its own counsel.
She has intended to make a fire for over an hour.
Instead, she has drunk coffee, balanced her checkbook,
bought a ticket for the faraway summer.

As the brightness dims, she stops staring at the floor,
lights a cigarette, urinates in the windowless bathroom
without switching on the light and walks into the living room.
Torn-to-size yellow paper in front of the fireplace

keeps her from going any farther. She wraps *What Work Is*
for her granddaughter who is three, decades away from reading it.
When dusk comes, she'll reach in the basket, taking only one log.
There will be no matches. She'll use a crystal lighter,
one that Greer Garson might have held in the forties.

The room yearns toward the simplicity of a pathway.
Clutter surrounds her like leaves from too many falls.
She wanders alone into the forest of her life.
These stacks of paper, this trail of crumbs.

✈ HAIRDRESSER

"Having created a cuckold, [Joyce] wondered how it felt to be one. 'Jim wants me to go with other men,' his wife reported, 'so that he will have something to write about.' She didn't greatly care for the idea and in the end was prepared to do no more for the cause of twentieth-century literature than address him in a note as 'Dear Cuckold.' This appeared to do the trick."

WILLIAM TREVOR

"In my more frivolous moments, I end up saying 'I love you' to whomever I'm speaking. I always mean it when I say it. That's the part I like best about frivolity."

PANKY HOLLEMAN

Conrad's Mother

Dell Horoscope says marital bliss is going to be Big in May.
I'm not married, have never been married
although I played at it once
with an intensity no wife would ever feel the need for.
I baked bread, breastfed the baby,
apprenticed myself to canning chow-chow
in the kitchen of a woman who knew what she was doing.
Conrad's mother could lift that iron lung of a pressure cooker
from off the wood stove with just one swing and two potholders.
Her corset arranged for her body to look like a barrel.
Dressed in tiny-flowered prints,
the bosom must have sighed each night when the bra came off.
Her feet lived modestly in black lace-up shoes
that could walk to kingdom come,
which was from the bedroom to the kitchen and back again 22,000 times
with sidetrips to church on Sundays and to the toilet
whenever she got lucky.

Party to a railroad husband and hard-drinking, scoff-law sons,
she was the only thing in the house
that was dependable. She worked every time.
She hadn't spent months on some layaway shelf
developing bad habits like the tv and radio.
Biscuits are relished by hungry men
even if the cook is as dull as a penny
in the pocket of a prison inmate who specialized in mayhem.
Given a richer husband, Conrad's mother would have had to entertain,
circulate cornbread and bean hors d'oeuvres,
chauffeur the sons to karate lessons.

In the supermarket parking lot tonight, Saturday night,
a bevy of teenagers are stacked over in the SE corner as if
they have just arrived at the trendiest nightclub on Sunset Strip.
A twenty-five-year-old and his twenty-four-year-old friend,
walking SE, never see me as they cut in front of my cart.
I hear King of the Jungle say to Cock of the Walk,
"The minute you have children,
you are gone, man. Good as dead.
Written off for the rest of your life."

A woman who lives alone
will go out at nine o'clock at night
to buy ranch dip for the carrots, cappuccino
truffle chocolates for the office, and yoghurt
even though they've taken the *h* out.

Dell Horoscope doesn't know the slightest thing about marital bliss.
It correctly guessed Conrad's mother would never buy its magazine
but it should have considered the odds
when counting on those women with baby carrots in their mouths.
The sharp snap of a broken root between the teeth
pleases the muscles in an unhappy face
about as much as anything can.

Pyramids, Rome, and Pharaohs

The oldest women in the U.S. are not the 100-year-old ones.
Some of us are 99 by the time we're 40.
After that is another century.

Bitterness settles in. All the accumulated humiliations
harden and dull the gleam of the chandelier heart.
Cirrhosis of the liver is nothing in comparison.

Things wait. Only when we're vulnerable
do they spring the surprise they've been saving for us:
How calculating the world is, how condescending.

In spite of our sunglasses, we see it:
Devotion to parents and all the best tables in restaurants
are reserved for the wealthy.

Having placed little stock in marriage, we burn midnights
taking self-styled classes in economics, poring over
how *widows* are the only hags with money,

how single mothers invariably squandered theirs on food,
cornets, shelter, ballet, clothing, cars, education, travel,
secular indulgences like karate lessons.

Inspectors condemn the blood-house, nail shut the doors,
post signs saying how unsafe it is inside.
Some of us think, *I could have told them that years ago,*

but disown our grown children instead.
Having abandoned *us* long before, they take no notice.
We send no word.

Condemned houses are haunted. *Something* lives in emptiness.
The pyramids, the mansions of Rome, the granaries of Pharaoh,
those citadels of the plunging neckline, gleam in moonlight.
If a woman is not Cleopatra, who owns Egypt?

Introduction

I must let you know who I am upfront?
No one stir fries who he is so that you can eat it hot.

When introduced, I do not say
Oh, mine was a common law marriage
and then rush to reassure you
– but it's printed up in Who's Who.
I do not whip out my receipt to prove
I paid as much for my divorce as you did for yours.

Nor do I announce
that, on my son's foot,
the fifth piggy went
Oui, oui, oui, oui, oui, Monsieur
instead of *whee, whee, whee.*
No normal pigs hung out around my child's feet.
I wasn't raising a prodigal son.

Nightmare and chaos have a right to be
what they are.
Everyone says I need to structure those years
which passed in a blur.
How could that help *then?*
In spite of my resistance to Gertrude's inch-thick lipstick
so that Pain can be the first whore to chair a committee,
I realize we pay little attention
to strangers who just start talking:

My friend and I were going home after the theatre.
A street person standing on the corner yelled at us.
I dismissed it as some ugly epithet a man stranded in the cold night

might well feel like yelling at a white Lexus streaking past.
Then, for some reason, I knew what he'd said.

I asked, *Are your lights on?*
Already in that nether world where ramps lead to freeways,
Alicia groped. *God, no!* traveled all the way up
from her conservative shoes. We were silent.
It takes time to absorb a humbling experience.

Necessity whispers behind the back of Scraped-Together Luxury
who carries a clutch purse pressed to her chest.
Cinderella had three mothers working for her.
Only one of them bad.
Only one of them dead.
Ophelia had none.
Women wrap themselves in fake fur
rather than give up being animal altogether.

So I am going to tell you who I am.
Wendell Berry said, *Be like a fox,*
who makes more tracks than necessary,
some in the wrong direction.

Each animal makes his own wisdom.
That man throwing himself across the night
at a car rushing past is who I am.

Working My Way Up

The acrobat on the entrepreneurial ladder is selling
himself to the highest rung tonight.
The somersault is best from there.

A teabag that's already been to tea
sags on the lip of the saucer.
The stain of its kiss comes too near the cup.
I keep telling myself,
Avoid restaurants too stingy to buy teapots.

The bookshelves in my apartment have become
a Missing Persons Bureau. You can spend
months looking for Joseph Conrad, never find him.

Timeless women are clueless.
David wants to argue with me,
*Referring to yourself as a woman in the past tense
isn't logical.*

I speak from limited experience
but I have things to tell David *and* Joseph.
To be female is to lie with the image of God.
It requires a certain tolerance
for fear, for trembling.

Passion takes away first your clothes,
then your self, then your country.
Time and space suck in their guts and disappear.
That's as close to genderless as you can get.
You're lucky if you don't end up
kissing your own arm by mistake.

Was Eden a Gated Community?

Crust, cup, flesh, flask.
Whirlwinds from the Gulf,
that horizon, this desert, your life.

The hag does not worry like the man from Baghdad.
She's not riding any horse to Samarra.
Worth noting: what gave in last.

Her heart dances for her when she lies down, folds
herself into darkness. Even though a coward,
she insisted on everything. Her guts are worn-out from it.

Her lungs still need smoke, visible proof
what air does when air is alone. Out of people,
the hands hold strips of eucalyptus bark and stones.

The heart doesn't want to go dead.
It wakes her one night as it fights against quitting.
She can feel blood spurting in the aorta,

inside and outside her skull, pounding out
the dancing beat of a drunken Brueghel party.
One drop of adrenaline on top of it could kill her.

Occasionally we know what we want
and we say it aloud. It's a prayer.
If you leave me alive, let me keep my brain.

I can't get along without it. Please, she says.
The prayer teaches her she has one last thing – her life.
To love it would be as exotic as a truck driver

quoting Bulgachov and Shakespeare.
She knows risk,
even succeeded at it once or twice.

This love would involve none, requires discipline instead.
Her high-kicking water legs counted on a future
even though she wore hairshirts.

Her calves are varicose maps, marked
with all the places she'll never go again.
Self-knowledge is useless. The self keeps changing

even after death. What lay beyond
the gates of Eden looked like that.
If the angel with a flaming sword likes to say

he chauffeured this woman out, that's his business.
The thing is the gates were thrown open.
And, for all I know, still are.

✈ TANNING BOOTH

"As a poet I must refuse to cooperate with the
committee on what I can only call aesthetic
grounds. The view of life which we receive
through the great works of art is a privileged
one – it is a view of life according to probabil-
ity or necessity, not subject to the chance and
accident of our real world and therefore in a
sense truer than the life we see lived all
around us."

THOMAS MCGRATH speaking before the
House Committee on Un-American Activities

"This place is all bowling alleys and howling
valleys."

PANKY HOLLEMAN

The Woman Who Wears Black Most Days

for Sue Pistole-Stuart, a high school teacher who was
described as "too intelligent" for the job

We have been concerned about our English teacher.
She gives us lessons in cursing the fig tree,
turning water into wine at weddings for Mother,
handling money changers in the temple, and drinking
water from a woman's cup.

She interrupts herself to write things on the board,
saying "Copy this in your notes."

The fingers of my feet rattle their wedding rings
when they know we are about to go somewhere.

Peas are good for you. Therefore, it's okay for the baby
to have three of them stuffed up her nostril.

Marrow runs out of my bones to form the island of Hawaii.
The con man has just asked some brunette to boogie
while a volcano is waltzing in natural catastrophe.
The burglar has tangoed his third house for the night,
leaving the TV, the thirty-inch world
that can't be sold to even a fence,
just the right amount of media coverage
for the disaster of my life.

Our teacher has a theory that fat people are trying to prove
they are here, skinny ones are not at all sure they want to be.
We are encouraged by the few pounds she has gained from
drinking bottles of Baileys. We imagine her growing larger,
in front of a window late at night, watching rain hit against the glass.

Books

When Grendel stopped going home, what did *his* mother do?
More mercenaries than Beowulf have been hired to fix me.

In her loneliness, my mother takes up inspirational books
written by opportunists of the Judas school.
Faces manacled in pious smiles,
not one of them is half my mother
but she's never gotten over what she didn't have.
She went no farther than the ninth grade in school.
Now, she could impress Socrates
yet seasons the moon like a pot roast.
Knowing my screams scare *me* half to death,
she sends copies of all she reads.
I never open the books. Neither do I throw them away.
To avoid desecrating my bookcases,
I hide the books in the hall closet as they arrive in twos and threes.

Sons eventually come home. To store boxes.
Males collect fantan dancers at universities and then
don't know what to do with them.
My son finds several five-foot-high stacks blocking his way.
"Why are you keeping hostages in this closet?" he asks.
"They're fake literary figures," I say.
His look says I don't know the first thing about being glib.
"Okay," I say, "they're wise men with sand in their shoes
and terribly lost. They thought a dollar sign was a star."

Like all sons since Cain and Abel, he makes his point.
After loading the car, I drive to Goodwill.
On my fifth trip inside, the woman at the scarred counter says,
"You've a lot of books, don't you?"

Embarrassed to be throwing a fit of heresy
in a town that loves God,
I say, "My mother gave them to me."
On my sixth trip, the woman shakes her head.
"Your mama sure wants you to be a good girl."

The 40 watt hallway bulb inside me lights up.
"Yes," I say.
In a Mary Magdalene way, I have been *good*
but more intense about it than my mother bargained for.
Wanting to help, I say, "You can always feed these to the lions."
The woman comes right back, "That's what any heathen would claim."
The counter goes through this transaction without a scratch.

Like Hamlet at his best, I sing out, "Good night, sweet ladies,"
with enough *good nights* thrown in to put Ophelia under water.

Books II

I put five books on the counter for check-out.
Laser busy in her hand, the woman laughs before she says,
"Did you know these are *all* by the same author?"
This is not a librarian, not even an aide, in front of me.

This is a dance floor. It's all cheek to cheek, pelvis to pelvis.
Her eyes tango straight toward me, two bandoneónes
inside her clothes stage front. The thin missile of the dancers'
straight-out arms has pointed flair. I watch for that kick, back and up,
to show off the leg. The right eye is a bookie out on the town.

The woman turns to the other woman behind the counter,
her left profile angled toward me. Another swirl and dip
are coming. "These books are *all* by the same author."
The other woman pretends she's too busy to hear.

The hilarity of the moment simmers down to a few
bubbles of glee. "Due June 16, in two weeks," she says,
privy witness to a shady Tijuana marriage.
I grab up my books and lean over the counter,
"Lady, I don't have a dime-a-dance mind."

She looks over my head, which is not that easy to do,
for the person behind me. It's a child with a swelter of books,
no two by the same author. Contender in the Zippity-Do-Dah
contest, he poses like a fisherman with his catch.

The glory nets of his ears hold still.
Gold stars swim in his eyes.

Postcard: The Geography of Mailboxes

Toward the east, the red mesas
have turned mauve and slate blue.
The sculpted doorway is not Stonehenge.
No one put it there except wind and rain –

tools that belong to God. A man with a patent.
Someone who knew advantages the minute he saw them.
The tough sagebrush like clumps of tender grass,
that bloodred rock, powder the minute it's touched…

the desert just lies there, a flat-bellied man,
the muscles relaxed as he sleeps.
But space is noticeable. It lures us forward
promising nothing in particular.

It knows how to show its worth:
details wiped out, aura turned up.
The edge of the earth touches the farthest cloud.
Walking off this hot sand onto the lush moss

of another world, we wouldn't even break stride.
Nothing is less a burden than our lives of *too little* have been.
On such wide land, we can feel that lifting up
which mesas do. They bear witness

to how light the sky really is, how close
to flying we are. Someone right now
is soaring into that distance, pumping his wings
until he feels the wind take over.

Gather at the River

I'm not into decor.
A white rug can get only so dingy,
but pictures of dust mites
scare me to death.
Who else do you know
produces a pile of shit
bigger than himself
at one sitting?
Do those pictures lie,
knowing alarm alone
will drive me into devoting
a whole day to a wet floor?

Growing up Southern,
you simply can't get rid of
Cleanliness is next to Godliness.
It's the *hook* from which
the carcass of any Southern mind hangs.
I don't resent this in the least –
this keeping it simple.
Cleansing is endless and tangible –
just what wrestling with the soul ought to be.
Plait that child's hair,
wash her face with a spit-wet finger.
Even strangers will love her instantly.
Suck that man's toes.
He'll not casually leave for foreign countries.
Lick your own arms any hot afternoon
to cool yourself off.

It's not a shower, a bath.
It's ablution, absolution,
pardon by the governor.
Jesus washing the disciples' feet
instead of giving a farewell speech.
Mary Magdalene coming
with her ointment and tears.
Her towel of hair.
A baby smelling of nothing
but his own flesh.
The sweaty excitement
of helplessness: lush with need.

So this day lost to patience,
to staying off a wet carpet
while it dries imperfectly through the afternoon,
comes before work, ambition, pleasure
— this rush of the river kissing your flesh,
this pulling the body awake
inside your Sunday clothes.
Hallelujah,
         hallelujah,
                  hallelujah.

Sitting in a Room

The windows above the french doors
do no more than the doors,
but they do it with more finesse.
The windows know something about romance.
You feel it in the neck,
the whole head lifting up and back
to meet the bold stare
before the kiss
runs its tongue along the flesh to study every pore.
The bones beneath feel the touch of it —
the rush
the flood
the blossom
the essential heat within
balanced against the sun.

No One Has Asked for My Word on Things

You're famous for getting your way. The sheer audacity
of what you say often wins for you. "There have never been
any boundaries between us." The lilt given certain words
suggests an extraordinary intimacy. Amazing how you'll lie
to even good friends. Barbed wire stretches out around us

in all directions, comes close up tight whenever we're in
the same room. Keeping out of the way of one spoke jams
me into the spike opposite. Roulettes of little knives do not
maim or kill, merely hurt and scar: *I have been here.*

Caligula is the only man I know of who knew no boundaries.
I think of the bronze bull in which a man could be roasted alive,
his screams rendered into a brave roar by an ingenious device.
Part of the entertainment at dinner that night, the designer of

this machine presented his creation to Caligula, to his drunken
guests. The machine-maker must have smiled when Caligula's
eyes gleamed. Having pleased an emperor, he wildly imagined
the rewards awaiting him: ruby ring, cellar of wine, *favor.*

In the annals of history should be the precise look on this
sucker's face when Caligula chose him for the bull's first victim.
Caligula showed the ruthless what ruthlessness really was.
Destroying natural boundaries first, he didn't upset anyone much.
His trampling on the club rules left all of them aghast.

I'm a woman, not a man. That's a boundary. I like the firmness
of the sea washing up on land. Sea and land come together in
a way two like things never can. Only one other man's flesh has

spoken to mine so surely, has ever come together with mine like the sea feeling solid shore. The barbed wire I could do without,

but it is a boundary the hand wants to touch, the mouth yearns to find. "There are boundaries between us." The flatness put in those words pulls back the rush of every wave I feel. Leaving the room is to get through the barbed wire fence unscathed.

Garlands

Her hand broken in three places, the little bones,
the ones that ripple underneath the skin along
the back. A field worker, she was picking table grapes.
A crate hurriedly placed on top of hers before she had
cleared her right arm. The doctor signs the release
for her to go back to work. One day in the fields and
her hand swells up twice its size. Her son
misses school again to drive her back
to the doctor. Showing him her hand, she
tells him, "I can't do the work." He says,
"Sure you can. Just use your hand *moderately*."

I am standing in the dry cleaners, talking
to the seamstress and the girl who works
the front counter. The seamstress has made
the mistake of asking how I am. The boy with
the field-worker mother has just told me this story
to explain his recent absences from class. When I
re-tell the story, the seamstress, steeped in every day
her hands have held needle and cloth, lets scorn
hiss out of her like a kettle. "There's no such thing
as *moderate* use of hands." The hispanic girl says,
"I've heard so many stories about that doctor."

For a moment, a garland of dark red flowers
and anemic pinks holds us in its ring.
We do not dance. We stand listening, hear a woman
being raped behind a door that, if opened, could stop
the screams. We falter. The garland falls from our hands.

We walk off into our lives, work our way down
dark streets alone, bones rippling underneath
our skin, bruised shadows growing larger.

✦ MANICURIST

"I travel light; as light, that is, as a man can travel who will still carry his body around because of its sentimental value."

CHRISTOPHER FRY

Beginning

Newly arrived in Chicago, living on Menomonee
just off Lincoln Park, we're at the corner of
Division and Clark, about to go into a poolhall
two doors down. It's a January 9:00 pm.

He's weeping suddenly, out of the blue or the beer,
having had both. He keeps saying,
"I'm a son of a bitch. I'm a son of a bitch."
I've seldom seen men cry but was taught

to pay attention to flickers of distant lightning,
to the twitch of a horse's flank ridding itself of flies,
to tightened muscles around the jaw. Something awful's
at work if men go that far. The confession has to do with me.

The fire in the crotch warms the chambers of the heart even
with the waist encircled by ice. Stranded on this Cocytus street
at 22, I'm his only witness. He made a promise I did not ask
of him. He lied. His anguish real for these moments,

I keep saying, "No. No, you're not."
Snow descends out of the sky, falls on our heads
in flakes of bliss. My fear is solid as the ice
on the sidewalk. Our inadequate shoes hold us there.

Later, I learn not to contradict a man when he speaks of himself.
He probably knows what he's talking about. Keeping my eyes
open in the dark, I ask *Why* before kissing atrocities
full on the mouth. Truth is as hard to hold as love.

43

Speaking to My Granddaughter

I

Your father calls to say you have been born.
Black hair and dark blue eyes.
"Ugly as a Chow with a bad attitude.
But growing beautiful by the minute."
As your grandmother, I've done my work.
I researched you. With great authority, I announce,
"She is Tuesday's child, full of grace,"
before siding with your mother about your ears.
"I can't believe you're saying this," he tells me.
"She can't grow up in Spain with unpierced ears." I say
it slowly so that the identity crisis he's going to cause will sink in.
He fumes, never having understood the consequences
of choices. (Neither did his father.) Filled with the wonder of you,
your father talks on and on. Before I can imagine your weight
in my hands, I must multiply 3.5 kilos by 2.2. He gives your length
in meters. My prowess with numbers is nothing to be genetic about.
Three days ago, he was reconstructing the half-forgotten words
of "I Gave My Love a Cherry" as he waited for you.

I cannot sleep. Inside my head, your name *Elena* repeats
like song notes needing their own history for a melody.
You are half a world away. It would take three wise men and a star
for me to get to you. That or a plane ticket from your grandfather.
Wise men and stars are more likely.
Only women never given a thing spend time thinking of gifts
that will not come. Unraveling myself from the covers,
I set out down the dark hallway to arrange your marriage.
When I turn on the kitchen table lamp, the wooden ball at the end
of its chain feels round as the world, cushioned in my hand.

We are old friends, have often made these late night forays together.
Not acquainted with many five-year-olds, I write Dylan in Oregon:

> *I know someone named Elena who might be*
> *the perfect wife for you. Her father is going to be*
> *very particular about whom she marries, but I think*
> *he would like you a lot.*
> *I got out of bed to write you this. Occasionally*
> *an outrageous woman turns out to be right.*

Another Irishman. You would think I'd learn. But people,
by and large, are stormy. Passion rides the high seas.
I want for you a harbor: Two people asleep in one bed,
their breath gentle against the other's skin. Knowing nothing
of witchcraft, I make it up as I go. Call me your *bruja.*
Jason called Medea that as he stroked the golden fleece.
One Christmas your father and I flipped a quarter to see if we would
go to Hawaii or buy him a pin-striped suit. Most other times,
we ate the quarter, took it on our tongues like the body of Christ.

I tell your father about the letter.
In a tone that says it takes everything in him
just to speak to me, he instructs me over the phone,
"Mother, don't do ridiculous things like that."

No one has ever liked my favorite lines. When I say,
Lady, I'm old enough to be dead, someone invariably
points out sotto voce, *But everybody is old enough to be dead.*
All those within earshot stay solemn
as Jehovah's Witnesses when I say
some Mexican village south of Atoka, Oklahoma.
Maybe if I said, *south of Canada,* someone could do
something besides worry about Texas and the Gulf of Mexico.

Your grandfather frequently referred to my mother
as "that ridiculous woman." It's not wise to use
that word on me. But your father's preface of silence
was worse. He's the only one who can flatten the earth,
push me to the edge of it. Weeks later, he calls
because I haven't. He tells me a story about himself:

II

Your father is sitting in the priest's office with his fiancée,
your mother. He's not Catholic. She goes to Mass
every day. The priest asks if he has ever been baptized.
The answer is *yes*. "When and where?"
the priest intones without looking up from the form
he is filling out. "I don't remember when but
I remember where vividly. In the bathtub
at my grandmother's house." The priest looks up.
"Who baptized you?" Your father's look is as
steady as the priest's. "My grandmother."
The priest fidgets with some papers on his desk.
He is a good friend of your mother's uncle.
They belong to the same Order. "If she said
the right words, it may count."
"Well, I really don't know her exact words –
I was underwater at the time – but I assure you
no one except John the Baptist could have done
a better job." The priest looks through the window
at the afternoon sky which threatens rain.
By *Baptism* for the groom, he writes *Questionable*.

Your father would have tried to jump the Grand Canyon
to marry your mother, yet he did not leave out his grandmother,
a hard woman to explain to a priest, to anyone.
I cannot believe my luck.

The emotions that crowd any heart lighten for a moment.
When I can speak, I tell your father,
"You are as beautiful as she was."

III

John baptized Christ. They were cousins. Keeping it
in the family like that, I'll baptize you, Elena McCarthy Ruiz,
in the name of the Father, the Son, and the Holy Ghost
off the coast of Sicily. Such simple words and the Tyrrhenian Sea.
I'll wade out, the sleekness of my thighs lost in the waves
just yesterday. You with your dark hair, in my hands tomorrow,
the brunette girl your great-grandmother mourned
when she looked in the mirror of her last years.
The Mediterranean will wet and salt your head.
The living and the dead will kiss your feet.

Talking to Elena

> And place is always and only place
> And what is actual is actual only for one time
> And only for one place
> T.S. ELIOT

Dante made hell a place. A monument to poetic justice:
the wings of Cocytus fanning the ice, keeping it solid
around his waist, caught forever in futile attempts at liberty,
at power. Trapped in my own impatience,
I feel the limitiations of my life.

Eliot made Ash Wednesday the space between blue rocks,
just enough room for three dreams to cross. Reminding us
of the white-gowned woman, he turned the leopards
albino, bestowed the beach and rolled trouser-legs upon men,
entrusted women with Michelangelo.
Transported straight from Missouri to England...
by way of Harvard and Cambridge and marriage.

I swam one winter in a mountain stream
with your grandfather. It was the first time for me
to give way to what is there in skin, to display my body
before any man. The luminous flesh with its capacity
for grace and humiliation. The sky above us
was a ravine of stars, the water alive with the shadows
of rocks and ruffled points of light. I swam out
to him, the icy water fluttering around our treading legs.

In someone else's apartment, before the days of air-
conditioned summers, we moved on the bed in unison,
the sweat on our bellies a rhythmic sucking noise,

one of the few times I knew love as a comfort. Wrapped around
another person like that freed me up to the rest of the world.
The animal ancestor that had galloped across plains knew
what was most me: the unconscious, unknown, unborn.

These are only two of the places that made you,
child of one year. I, who have felt the moist palms
of your hands only once, tell you this.
You will never know how poignant your back looks
to your father as you walk away. The only path you have
lies between where you came from and where you stand.

Love is an animal in the solitude of rain.
When you halt, wet in the cold wind,
may God raise his fist and strike our hearts.
May they break into caves and give you shelter.
May the wilderness of memory feed you flesh.

Reading at the Tujunga Library

The first thing I do is whip into the restroom. It's a characteristic of those who drive from Bakersfield. You can spot us in any crowd.

On the door of the toilet stall, written with a black magic marker at the end of the 20th Century, is the room's only graffito:

MARTHA FERGUSSON

IS A WHORE

That old black magic...that I know so well.

The one Biblical word left in this secular world still owns all its veils, still knows the hootchie-kootchie. There's a Herod behind every Salome.

I once said to a man as we sat on a front porch of a farm house near Pidgeon Forge, *You don't act as if you want a wife and a baby. You act as if you want to be single again.* He looked out across the small valley toward the Smoky Mountains, then looked at me. He said, *I guess that's right.*

I had two arms and a baby. I could afford one suitcase. I packed it. Wanting to be in charge of this departure, he came in to help me plan. I let him. It's a great failing on my part. I don't plan. I come. I go. He bought me a train ticket to Wyoming. He insisted on Wyoming, on removing me from everything I had ever known.

Just before I left, he raised his eyebrows in consternation and asked, *But what will you do? Be a whore?* I tried to burn the mattress. I tried to pull it outside and burn it on the front lawn. The landscape around Cheyenne made me feel as if I were on the moon.

I don't know who Martha Fergusson is. But I wish her a *lot* of success. So much...she has to have a yard sale to get rid of some of it...so much...she has to become a philanthropist to keep the IRS from impounding her...so much...*success*...that all the magic markers in the world know her name by heart.

⤷ PLASTIC SURGEON

"Only what is impervious to our scheming
offers the mind the bewilderment it seeks,
the repose in wonder."

TIM PARKS

Geology of Home

I never thought I'd send you a present.
...Come to think of it, I've sent you several.
No one with an ear for voice can help but love this book.
Mountains have their effect. They did on us.
I like the way the old man believes no one but a cloven-footed
Devil could've taken his newborn son.

He made me homesick for the Hawke Community graveyard.
My mother took me there sometimes to visit
her mother's grave, the other Burton graves.
But never until I was grown, had moved away,
knew what it meant to be bereft.

Hawke Community stopped existing long ago.
The cemetery is edged with woods. The families
of the people buried there let most of the woods come
in, but mow the grass and keep the briars cut back.

It's a countryside scourged by farmers looking for new land,
by lumber mills. The oldest cedars and oaks in the county
shade the cemetery. On hot days, no breeze stirs even
the highest branches. Even though the land is
flat and nondescript, the silence can be immense.

When the old man in the book talks about *blood*, he sounds
like my mama. She always figured the Burton blood
would save me from the Holleman blood. She married into
a mean-spirited family. My daddy had her entire sympathy
for being related to such people. She was probably nicer
to all of them than they were to each other. She thought,

if generosity walked around, it rubbed off on people. A woman
can bend herself to making the world what she wants it to be.

My mother's life was so much turmoil, a dirt road with too many
potholes, the powdery dust roiling up behind and over her.
But when I stood in that graveyard next to those woods and felt
the soft ground give under my feet, I knew the land she did
when she was a girl and rode bareback through the woods.

The wild girl still inside her belonged to the land and the land
belonged to her. Never without animals, she took care of
Tennessee Walkers, tiger cats, Dobermans, yellow chicks.
She knew how to kill cottonmouths, to nurse a sick calf.
My sister and I grew up with baby rabbits salvaged
from rice fields and a red-tail fox orphaned by a threshing machine.

Poverty made her angry the way children made her stern —
both states to be out-grown as soon as possible.
Only if something made her laugh could she accept it for
what it was. She took me with her to visit old men and women.
Only now do I realize most of those people were related to me.
Some of them simply had known her mother.
Wherever she went, I went. Whatever was hers was mine.
Except when her father Noah died. She shared that with no one.
We were cut off by her face: tight lips, eyes turned inward.

According to her, the last funeral at Hawke Community was
hilarious, the grown children complaining about the dust, the heat,
the mosquitoes. Furious their father had insisted on being buried
there, a long way from anywhere. She enjoyed telling it.

My mother knew how to pull the texture of land in
through her nostrils, hold it in her head.
Maybe everyone does that, but she's the one who taught me how,

taught me to do it. And that is why I loved you.
You did it quietly the way she did.

II

You and I were not well-matched. Yet that is also what you loved
in me without your knowing it. I was watching a torrent of rain
in Chicago through the window once. You called me back.
I looked so lonely sitting there you said. But you suspected
nothing of me was left in the room and you were jealous then,
afraid that I could disappear as totally as you into what had
no form, what had motion but was no more than sound or smell.

When I go home, I put a dozen roses on my mother's grave
beside my daddy's. He must still groan over the willful extravagance
of the true-to-the-bone daughters of his wife. The roses wilt
within an hour. They are for the part of my mother that's dead.

But when I want my mother, she stands beside me
looking at the gravestone of a stillborn, the child
my grandmother Melissa died giving birth to, my mother twelve.
Within a year, my grandfather married the widow
Ruth who favored her own children over his.

They were married in two buggies between Vanndale
and Cherry Valley. The minister met them at that halfway point.
He did the ceremony from astride his horse. It was winter and cold.
My mother cooked the wedding supper for the two of them,
then left the house to sleep at a neighbor's.

III

Separately but both there, we watched our son be married.
Above the stone floor of the Cathedral of Guadalupe,
he had the Romantic wedding we never did.
The bride's mother wore emeralds from Colombia.

Among the guests in their best jewels, glistening stones
from dark places in the earth, I was plain as mud.
We were half a world away from Hawke Cemetery,
from the woods that guard the softness of the ground there.

The other presents...I sent you pictures of Chase's childhood,
a childhood you never witnessed but must have felt.
Cut off from the land with so little real except inside him,
Chase had no way of feeling you. He must have ached to know
you the way I ache now remembering Hawke Community.
I'm not that strong a woman, but I think you supposed I was.
My mother left me soft as the earth she loved.

She gave up riding horses when she was thirty-five.
But at seventy-two, with paralysis overtaking her, she returned
to horses. An old woman on an old horse as surely as
a girl on a young mare. She said over the phone,
"Dear, don't think of me as ill.
Think of me as riding, as part of the wind."

Larger than I Am

I

I want to sit in someone's lap, someone much larger than I,
the feel of his hands on me,
his voice deeper, more sure of itself than mine.
I want him to tell me absurd stories, sing me sad ballads,
teach me games for which I'm not expected to show any skill.
For him to shoot craps with me on the bedroom floor,
as my father did. When he had no pennies, we bet
the kitchen matches carried in his pocket.

II

The large hand of the body is the lap. The crotch
milks a penis but does not cradle semen. It drips out.
The bladder, anus get rid of food and drink.
The mouth bubbles words out of itself, tries to empty
the brain of mystery. Pores sweat on the sly. The nose
blows snot. The body absorbs but gives it up later.
Only the lap holds a thing without trying to dissolve it.
Only a lap cherishes, takes comfort from otherness.

III

My mother had me against doctor's orders, my coming
dangerous. I was to be a boy. Before going to
the hospital, she ate an entire mince pie. The first
five miles of the sixty-mile trip were gravel road in
December, 1938. With her in full-blown pain, my father
stopped the car to light a cigarette. His hands
were shaking. My mother never forgot it.
The clean look of my bald head did not hinder her.
The long hair you see now was an act of her will.

She named me after Botticelli women, carried me as
an infant on a pillow, spared me her bony legs.
The woman knew how to focus.

IV

I want to be held in that large hand reserved for
newborn animals insistent upon moving around with
their eyes shut, sesame seeds which would be lost
between fingers, stones that need to touch each other,
to have a pale background for their strong, pure colors.

V

He was a drinker. My sitting in his lap
cut off the circulation in his legs.
Years later, a doctor amputated.
Arriving in Cayucos one Christmas, ready
to be repulsed, I found it second nature
to comfort what no longer was.
I massaged his stump.

The Visit

There's no evidence of the birch table in my mother's kitchen,
no evidence of the two coffee cups she's set out before she calls my name,
no vivid, frazzled roses cut this morning from her yard.

There's just a pair of bony, taut-skinned clouds like the backs
of my mother's hands that she would hold palms up across the table
as a way of showing who she was, that it survived distance and loneliness
as palpably as it lived in this silent clasp of flesh over shining wood.

I kissed the hands of both my parents as a child. I never outgrew it.
They were people who worked off the passions of their minds and hearts
through their hands as if trinities were necessary, existed everywhere.
They created chocolate pies and rice crops, placed them
in the v-shaped wake of Nothing as if it were a cornucopia.

The only light left in the curtained sky comes up from below,
a single spotlight thrown upon two tendrils of cloud.
I must turn in my carseat at the stoplight to keep the southwest in sight.
I roll down the winter-dirty window,
pull off my glasses, lean my head out.

From the darkness of this street, I watch the veined hands
reach across the sky.
The red light is kind. It holds these lines of cars in place,
thorned stems of roses.

Wife of Polonius

His good looks ruined his life, even as a child.
In those days, they didn't turn a court page
out on Wall Street to slay dragons after a term or two.
Once favored, there was nothing to do but promote him.
He knew too much.
And Polonius was such a guileless man.
They could count on his deceits being obvious.
No matter what went on, they knew, with him around,
they looked *transparent*,
several notches better than *honest*.
Like the plaited tresses of Gertrude,
they could track him
even amidst distractions and amusements.

He loved his children.
He just didn't have any skills.
When the FBI wouldn't oblige,
he hired a free-lance spy to investigate his own son.
Polonius got so used to doing business
he forgot himself.
Laertes and Ophelia loved him, but they
didn't suffer from illusions about how useful
"Neither a lender nor a borrower be" was.
They took care of each other. Then he sent
Laertes off to college, kept Ophelia home.
It was *custom*. We all know
how much *that* meant to him.

I could have forgiven him Ophelia
but he left her an absolute orphan.
He was hauled off like a sack of potatoes.

Of course, he had no business in Gertrude's bedroom.
Hamlet thought it was the King.
Who else would he expect to be hovering
behind the Queen's skirt?
Polonius prided himself on going beyond
everything except the tapestry.
He was a man fond of muffled sounds.

There my poor daughter was: Hamlet
acting crazy for months, then suddenly
gone, her daddy murdered,
her brother in the land of Higher Learning.
Polonius had told her to forget
about marrying up, but you can be sure
he didn't dash the hopes of Laertes.
In the land of elected Kings? No.

Gertrude and Claudius were fond of Ophelia –
everyone was fond of Ophelia –
but she embarrassed them.
Their crazy son had murdered *her* father
and *they*, more or less, were pretending
several people had never existed.

So what if Polonius wasn't a Horatio?
If *anyone* did Polonius's job for forty years,
you don't think he'd end up a blithering idiot?
After a few years of being Polonius at the UN,
Adlai Stevenson died out on the sidewalk,
his heart gone berserk. Imagine how
brilliant his regret.

I'm never even mentioned, but that means nothing.
How do you think Lear got his three daughters?

Ordered them out of a Neiman Marcus catalogue?
When boys play at being women,
you're going to have a lot of dead mothers.

Shortly after my death, Polonius got fat.
I'm what held him in balance.
I raised those sweet children of his.
But he stooped to using Ophelia on Hamlet
as a trap. Forced Laertes into the waste
of revenge. No, Polonius is in hell.
And I don't miss him. He never remembered
me to the Queen, to my children.
He thought he was sufficient unto himself.
And wherever do you think such people go?

Answering Back

Use mud. Use feathers that have fallen
to the ground of their own free will.

Silence is what you rub on the scar.
The scar does not go away but softens.

What works best is a silence that moves
at the slightest touch from the wind.

Healed and scarred, you cut wood thin, weave
strips of it into baskets. In the baskets,

you place artifacts of the old self. These
cradles fit on the shelf of the back closet.

On certain days, you turn on the closet light
to look through the baskets. What flows

out of the wounded spirit? Not blood.
What does the spirit wear? Not flesh.

If the arm of a lover choked you to death,
the spirit would not care. Coming at midnight,

it dances before you. Promising nothing,
it puts the blind art that made you yourself

into your hands. Silence moves around.
Looking down, you see dried mud, an array

of unmatched feathers, softer and more
capable than you ever wanted to be.

✈ ETIQUETTE BOOK

"What god would ever pander to the way
man saw things?"

TIM PARKS

Taking Conspicuous Consumption on the Road

Born in Spain, living in Berlin,
Elena McCarthy Ruiz
is out there dazzling the universe.
To speak to this baby
is a hard-talking job.
I've bought from Taiwan
two cats that meow,
two horses that neigh,
two pigs that oink,
two cows that moo,
two dogs that woof.

Elena and I each have a set
of these fuzzy, stuffed creatures.
(Even the pig has fur. Pink fur.)
Leading animals out of my closet of a barn
every Saturday morning,
I head for the phone.
Swinging on my arm down the hall,
the plastic bag goes off like a package
of mellowed-out firecrackers.
I ask my son to put the receiver
near Elena. As he does, all that is
in my heart pours across the country,

the Atlantic and half of Europe
into the more arctic zones of Germany.
Moo, it says.
Meow, it says.
Woof, it says.
Oink, it says.

Elena's mother is passionate about horses.
I squeeze my stuffed one three times,
its peal of whinnies
a concession to this child's being
someone else's besides my son's.

"Have you lost your mind?" he says.
"What is she doing?" I ask.
"She looks startled." He pauses.
"But interested." His cautious laughter
turns giddy. Three dharma bums
traverse space, the bark and purr
of this earth trailing behind them
like a comet's tail
as they round the bend into
Steppenwolf's spinning universe.

Real Estate

Fathers are forgivable.
Alcoholic mothers can get by if a beautiful hand holds the glass.
But abandoned mothers are dust.
Trying-to-do-it mothers are worse than cancer and lyme disease
        combined.
In this fertile country, everyone is self-made.
As far as having mothers, most prefer not to.

My son home for the rare visit,
I pull out the absolute total of my worldly estate:
restaurant food, a movie, grapes in the frig, disposable razor,
a long sofa, a new shower curtain.
Scoured tub, tangerine juice, echinacea for whatever ails him,
the results of my brain's waving to itself.
Dogs have gnawed my bones,
but being oh so literary, I've saved one or two to throw him.

From Amanda in Glass Menagerie
to Mary in Long Day's Journey into Night,
mothers are despised in this country.

Mothers come off well in literature, he counters.

American, I say. *Name one.*

Well, not off the top of my head in fifteen seconds.

Then I'm describing a famous poet's stumbling
and da-da-ing his way through the house that Jack built.
My son's eyebrows shoot up. He's about to be rhetorical.
You asked about mothers in literature?

His hand caught up in its handsomest gesture, on the table a straight flush,
Mother Goose, he says.

She's English, dear.

He tucks his chin and gives me a look
he's acquired since having a daughter.
It's a criminal lawyer's look,
of no use whatsoever in poker games.

We see *Bulworth* later in the day.
Without comment, he allows me to stomp both feet
when the movie gets happy, squirm during the more trying parts.
I bend forward for the dancing, elbows on knees, hands up to brace
        my head,
and push back hard in the seat when I need to get away from what's ahead.
Those around us assume he's come to the show with a lunatic.
Of course, it could be his American mother.

His patience is infinite.
A Chagall was behind the rocking chair where he was lulled to sleep
        each night.
I never floated off into the sky
even though a top-hatted fiddler plays Cicero, washboard polkas
in the left-over wing of my heart.

Talking to People You Can't See

Sometimes I want to lie down and die.
Important stuff never does this to me.
Pettiness reeking from the cavern of some human heart
is what takes my breath away.
Those days I'm down to two skills: I can walk. I still talk.
Living close to my last step, my last word,
taught me how to care for my young.

> Do you know anyone in the Wellesley area
> who's looking for a $1600 car?
> If you do, call my son.
> Lured to Boston by false claims of plentiful work,
> he looked like an Okie arriving in California.
> Similar to his mother's stepping off a bus in Lyman, Wyoming,
> suitcase in one hand, baby in the other.
> My son's moving back to Spain
> where unemployment has become
> an Art form: Less is more.
> His wife and child are there.
> If you know a buyer, the area code's 617.
> After that, you're on your own.
> If I gave you his number, he'd hate me for it.

The correct position for speaking
to people you can't see is on your knees.
The person who designed the phone booth
didn't throw himself into his job.
The whole concept came out of watching
lawyers plea-bargain in court.
Once my knees are down there, the only word
that makes any sense is "Please!"
The person I'm talking to
is supposed to know the details already.

But I'm not sure God speaks English.
Esperanto never caught on.
Latin might work but did the Romans ever say *Please?*
I'd take up foot-washing,
snake-handling,
if I thought they'd do any good.

Gifts are treble clef.
The marketplace is bass.
Your hands strike chords in both
worlds stretching out from middle C.

                             That's why I've called.
Sweet chariots swing high and then they swing low.
It takes a singer to get a ride home.

What Hester Prynne Told Young Women
Who Came to Her as an Expert on Trouble

Never let a man pack you off
to wait for him
among a slough of Puritans.
Never love a man who's a coward,
who's the darling of his Crowd,
who adores a far-off God
but can conjure no compassion
for a stranded woman.

Regret nothing.
Stitch your own *A*.
Wear it across your breast.
Let people assume it's for *Adulteress*.
They'll end by believing it's *Able*.
They'll never guess *Arthur*,
never think *Alpha*.

Regret nothing.
Call your children pearls.
Keep them away from swine.
Let them know the price they cost you
down to the Nikes on their feet and the wounds in your heart.
Otherwise, you leave them unprepared for life.

Regret nothing.
Remember always how your young,
lean body cried out for one man.
Let the body remember for itself
each time it was treated like a piece

of used furniture in a thrift store,
its back against the wall, to be had
for a single stroke of tenderness.

Never go with a race car driver
who has dimmers on his lights.
Don't be fooled by the white silk scarf
draped around his neck.
He's not a pilot.
Steps leading up to any scaffold
give men vertigo.

Regret nothing.
Keep a detailed map of
where you've never been
in your deepest pocket.
Stand on the earth.
Travel against the wind.
Bow down to nothing.
As if all that space
were your home,
kiss the sky.

Bruised Waters

Escaping a dungheap of workbooks smudged in the margins,
I smoke in the alley behind this building where I work,
a purveyor of math, English, all the sciences,
economics, government, history, fine arts, driver's ed.
No one has asked me to sing yet.
Or teach zither. Oboe. Kettledrums.
My student is in there writing about *A Place You Have Lived and Liked the Best*.
He's busy choosing Blackwell's Corner over East Los Angeles.
I agree with him. Space is everything.

The alley flooded, I sit in one of the lawn chairs I have landscaped
both mud and dust with. A car upholstery shop is neighbor to the
            swarming bees
which have housed themselves inside the rotted corner of the building.
Across the way is a welder's shop for farm machinery on the lam.
The men who come and go sometimes acknowledge my presence
but more often don't.

This morning the chair and I are secure on the concrete stoop
outside the peeling-paint door.
The makeshift pool of water at my feet reflects the sky.
An all-night rain has added this luxury of Japanese gardens.
White, pale gray, and dark clouds circle the sun, then
pass over. A white cloud is sucked loose from the others
by the sun's heat, erotic motion in the rush of it.

The sky goes down for miles within this inch or two of rain,
water giving a wavery depth to the world that air never would.
That's how sailors saw mermaids. It happens to us. Three-fourths
of the earth covered by water and we, brought to our knees,
see the sky. What we know, looking like a miracle.

→ COSMETICS IN THE PURSE

"A school board meeting was held for the
express purpose of denouncing a teacher who
had unsuspectingly chosen an obscene book
—John Gardner's *Grendel*. There were 150 of
them. And one of her. They had the Ministe-
rial Alliance on their side. She was a 115 lb.
woman whose hair needed shampooing. The
meeting went on for hours. Remindful of
what it was like before the advent of bath-
tubs, John Gardner had one old woman smell
of stale urine. A Board member thought that
taught high school seniors disrespect for the
elderly. The teacher was compared to Com-
munist China and the criminally insane.
Everyone chipped in and did his part. As one
man took the floor, he turned to face her and
said, 'There's filth in this world, true enough,
but we don't run it in our streets. We run it
in sewers under our streets where it belongs.
Excrement doesn't belong in a school.' All she
could think of was how much shit possibly
lay in the 151 coiled sets of intestines present.
She didn't think the man would like her
mentioning it, though. In fact, it might be
the very thought that would prove to them,
beyond a doubt, she was depraved."

PANKY HOLLEMAN

The Cuckoo Doesn't Know When to Come Out

> ...after centuries of internecine upheaval, treachery and
> violence, the Italians produced Leonardo da Vinci and
> the glories of the Italian Renaissance; after centuries of
> peace and brotherly love the Swiss gave the world the
> cuckoo clock.
>
> WILLIAM TREVOR*

Abrasive enough to clean out a bathtub,
I clog my way around the unlikely wish for birdbaths
in English gardens. Holding *Harper's* open
with my elbow, I order three bird clocks:
Are you sure the American robin
feels like singing at 1:00 in the afternoon?
Put me down for the frame that's green as a forest.
Walls wear clocks like hearts on their sleeves.
The sleeves should be fickle, envious, evergreen.
Do you guarantee a nightingale?
I need to hear birdcalls in my sleep.
My neighbors need to hear an eagle scream
when they sit down to dinner
but I'm not sure when they eat.
The woman on the phone
lets me twirl at my own speed.
Windmills creak in the background.
It seems comets have stopped persecuting the Dutch.

Splurges disappear in a flash of tail feathers.
By the time the package arrives,
I haven't a clue what's inside.

* William Trevor attributes the expressed sentiment to Graham Greene's *Third
Man*. Trevor thought it worth noting that Greene chose to be buried in
Switzerland, not Italy.

The cardboard smells like an empty nest,
but the return label keeps cheeping:
Fulfillment Company. I slit the top,
intrigued by what happy opera might look like.

Getting the clocks out of the box
is worse than trying to steal the bell
out of the Campanile.
To set the time requires
the same concentration Dreiser used
aligning his chair with the universe.
Matching the right songs with the right birds
takes the hands through the day's repertoire:
housefinch for noon and midnight,
southern mockingbird for 2:00,
bluejay for 4:00. The northern oriole
prolongs his sweet warble at 6:00.
Every hour has feathers.
Emily would be pleased.

I go to bed full of expectations, but things change.
Propped on the bookcase in my bedroom,
the clock is tickertape
going crazy over a stock market crash.
With a cane and one leg shorter than the other,
a phantom of the opera thuds around in a circle
as if he's conjuring a spotlight of darkness for himself.
He's working so hard,
my calf muscles cramp from helping him.

Hearts can break: Light-sensors aren't nocturnal.
These birds don't sing out in the dark.
I'm never going to hear nightingales.

The consolation prizes of my life
are coffee and tangerine juice.
The mourning dove sounds
much like a pigeon as I go out the door
to a job I've loved and hated for thirty years.
A career designed by *El Hombre sans Merci*.
Fine arts flit from branch to branch
above the bleak landscapes of public schools.
Dead tree limbs have no leaves
but insects are plentiful.
You just need to be a woodpecker
to get to one of them.

I return the two clocks meant for gifts,
hold onto mine. Trills are fragile.
I'm tolerant of whatever feels like quitting.
No bird calls out forever.

In summer, the sun floats and floats before it sinks.
From the plum trees near the window,
thrushes answer the birds on my bookcase.
We sail to Byzantium however we can.
With only two notes of a song,
the cuckoo emigrated from there.

Mailer wrote about the naked and the dead
like a Russian and became a famous man.
Melville sailed with Ahab, Ishmael, Queequeg,
died bitter and alone and broken.
Collecting butterflies, Stein knew Lord Jim.
Solid as afternoon light slanting across the floor
in an empty room, timeless moments happen.
We roll up our sleeves and wear them.

The Muses Have Moved In

It started out a French château right in the middle of Birmingham
but now papier-mâché snakes slither among the myriad chairs
on the ceiling of the foyer. Boxes of dynamite are stacked

on the dining table, illuminated by enough red candles
to burn down the house. Cave drawings hunker under the stairway
with a baboon's skull dressed up in his own fur bonnet.

An elephant foot has planted itself in the living room, along with
a Frank Gehry chair and a stuffed burro whose baskets
are filled with New Guinea masks and shields. Zebra rugs,

with one North American bearskin thrown in, are everywhere.
My foot hesitates to step on the manes protruding from the floor.
While red neon flows from several places including the kitchen,

a 1957 Chevy convertible door hangs over the toilet and Vulcan
revolves across from a Mussolini version of the three witches.
All of it manages to live together because of Louise Nevelson.

The husband says, "I like it. It wouldn't seem like home
any other way." She says, "We hope people
don't stop coming to our parties, though." It has taken

all this to replace three Alabama boys with extra-long legs.
Kids who could never stay in place come home now
to toast holidays and third world excursions.

No one is going over the brink. That's the point in form.
In aesthetics. In patronage of the Arts.
Nothing disappears. The stage looks stunning.

No one is striking the set. No one is pitching a fit.

Being Terrific

Teaching Lear and Shylock for years,
I knew in my blood they were true
but I didn't know mothers got it, too.
My imagination collapsed at the
thought of living long enough to be old.

Even the sow who ate her farrow is gone.
There's nothing in front of me —
nothing to mirror the face, the behind-your-back world,
no crystal ball future.
The last phase of the moon is paltry stuff,

but I was never any good as the jeune fille,
the cheerleader, the prom queen,
the career woman, the voluptuous femme fatale,
the devoted mother, or even the respectable matron
capable of a decent hand of bridge.

Although raised to be a lady, I failed to acquire the requisite
prissiness for it. I was soon called a fallen woman.
Withered edges growing from nature trails into boulevards,
I am turning into a full-blown hag.
The Miltonic plunge into this haven of ugliness
and gnashing of teeth surprises everyone.
It occurs to me I was born for it.

Last Phase of the Moon

Where I eat lunch, I have learned to be tolerant of
the occasional string at the bottom of my soup.
They have a patio where I can smoke.

Lottie regales me with anecdotes about her grandson,
all the stories indirect bragging but that's expected,
unlike the string hanging from my spoon.

Teams abound in this town.
No life exists otherwise. People without shadows
are suspect. The husband Hap takes my order.

As ice clunks into the styrofoam cup in my hand, I answer
Monday's question, "Oh, I'm moving
into my hag phase, and I think I'm going to be terrific at it."

Tentative laughter answers me.
"I wasn't much good at…" I look for something
that's not French. "The cheerleader type" would

work fine, but before I can finish, Hap says,
with his eyebrow raised, "Not much good at being
a *young hag?*" I study this man of wit for a minute.

"Oh, I was *excellent* as a young hag.
I just wasn't *popular* at it, that's all."
I fill my cup: lemonade, rootbeer, orange gunk, Diet Coke,

Dr. Pepper, and Mr. Pibbs – a carbonated witches brew
the better to bubble with, my dear –
and hunker-prance out to the patio where

Sally the cafe cat waits for my hamburger soup.

Bruised Waters II

It's Saturday morning,
one of the two mornings I have.
January sits outside the door,
its tongue numb from licking
the licorice-flavored snow cone
of last night.

Thinking of my son in Madrid
causes an ache
in my arms.
If I phoned him,
my face would glisten
with the sticky sap
that runs out of trees
before they die.

I've never seen
where he lives
but he's told me *small*.
A big man, he does not fit
into small.
The grace of his body
taken from him,
he moves there
with his head bent
as if he were in Plato's cave,
slowly turning
into the allegory of his own life.

Anything is better
than Manhattan.

But I know small.
He grew up in small.
It's not something
you look at a lot
but you feel it around you,
pressing against your flesh.
My son's gained weight.
Life-preserver fat
makes a husband safe,
undesirable
to other women.

His life is caught up
in a swirl of gonads and money,
— husband, father, work.
The shadows on the wall
tell him
that calculation suits him,
that he will escape
the obscurity his mother
struggled against.
Bereft of family and money,
she was left a moving target.
She held his hand,
hid his blond head
behind the billows of her skirt.

II

The talent for
colonizing dies hard.
In Madrid, they'd prefer
an orphan for a son-in-law,
but one mother is easy enough
to cut out of someone's life.

My son belonged
to himself
at age three.

The darkest spots of blue
in the never-still
waters of the world...
The flesh
does not bruise
until after the blow.
No ocean, no sky,
no cave, no fire,
no scatter of leaves given the wind
and received by the ground
has ever appeared
for sale
on any game board
called colony
called monopoly
called Franco
called Guernica
called Barcelona
called Lorca
hands tied behind his back
called mi hijo
mi hijo mi hijo.

Arrival

The pale red of sunset frames a city of clouds.
Its skyscrapers would please even a Romantic.

Driving west, I watch darkness run down the hills and settle in the dry riverbed beside the highway. Although night has cupped its hand over my car, it is still daylight in the distance where the ocean begins. A bank of clouds rises from the horizon.

I watch those cars that have paid a visit to this soft-as-a-llama city, the place of curved miracles, of desires only the sky could satisfy. The lights of the cars going east look no happier for having been down boulevards lined with trees foliaged in wet, white vowels. The cars look like fireflies trying to find each other in the dark, the silent whisper of their hidden wings a tangible part of the night.

We never know the mystery of where we are, only the mystery of where we're going. The wet, cold air outside my window smells of the ocean. Radiant even in winter, the western light says goodbye to the sun without knowing that it is saying goodbye to itself. The gathered clouds press against the parted lips of hill and coast.

Nothing beckons me onward. All of it says, *Be still. Soft rains will build this city over and over. It comes to you more than you can ever go to it. It's there in the way flesh cushions bone.*

HAG HOUSE

"If it begins to mean something, I can't help it."

SAMUEL BECKETT

"A high school counselor gave me an essay, saying she thought I might find it interesting. The piece talked about how common child abuse was and about how many children simply blocked all memory of it. In the middle of the article, Bryan James said, 'How do you know if you are emotionally damaged? It is very likely if you find yourself reacting to other people or external events a lot.'

I've taught for thirty-five years. I suppose the hope was I'd eventually fit in. The counselor's hand-out caused me to talk aloud to myself which, according to some sources, isn't a healthy sign. 'Is comatose the ideal?' I wanted to know. The next time I saw the counselor, I said, 'Art should get down on its knees every night and thank God for damaged people. We'd never have a standing ovation without them.' There I was, reacting again."

PANKY HOLLEMAN

The Vessel Won't Hold Water

Broken women have jagged edges. Ruins are
known by what's left. Who could have predicted
which walls would give way, which remain?

I walk over lumps in the road —
ruts of dried mud from a wet time. Gravel
crunches in its stubborn way under my shoes…

makeshift boulevard for a woman edged in
her own grainy, raw silk skin. The sun marks
as its own the bridge of my freckled Indian nose,

the cliffs of my bone-filled shoulders.
Quirky places of seduction, of intent gone home.
Watch out for lewdness, for the sensual swarm

of my arms wanting to embrace the heat of the
entire sky. Reaching all the way to Ireland
if it were *up* instead of flat on the earth,

I learn the nature of air.
This caress
runs hot and cold.

Mother of Jonah

That woman writhed every time he came up for promotion.
The professional ups and downs of prophecy were awful.

Wading in knee-deep, she wrung her hands and asked every
top-water fish sucking air, *Jonah, honey, are you okay?*

She could do nothing to save him. How did that little fact
hang next to her skin? She must have blistered and peeled

the night of the storm, felt rope-burns in her eyes, the ones
which scarred the hands that threw her boy overboard.

Back in the belly of things, he gave her no thought
although God must have been on his mind quite a bit.

Having succeeded in going where no one knew his name,
he spent all his time asking God to remember it

while she listened to rumors: burning bushes, balked donkeys,
even whales. She saw warnings, read signs, but could only

stand on the beach like a rock and wait him out. If God taught
Jonah to embrace his fate like a bride, God never showed him

how to lift the veil. But the job of delivering bad news was,
after all, a job. Enough to keep him in the marketplace.

Wedged between generations, the mother lived on
unleavened bread in the hills, held salt on her tongue.

Her silence, like the bell of a trumpet, flared out
with predictions not even God wanted to hear.

The Journey: What We Take with Us

They are four years old. He is her first friend, close as she'll ever
come to a brother. They teach each other to trust people.
Not wrong that first time, they'll be wrong almost every time

afterward. He inspires her one fist fight. The way first-graders
will do, Walter Louis Rose calls him a coward and other names.
Marching around the schoolhouse, four or five children

behind her as entourage, she hurls words at Walter Louis Rose's face.
Walter Louis throws one punch, knocks the wind out of her.
The surprise of not being able to breathe opens up

a whole world to her — that one person can do this to another.
In second grade, Robert gets the measles. On her way home
from school, she reads to him despite the dark of his bedroom.

He bribes her to stay longer than she's allowed to. When his tall, thin widow
of a mother gets home from work, she spoons up lime jello, chocolate
            pudding,
a different treat every day to counter the sameness of the afternoons.

He listens to her voice, not the words, and falls behind a grade.
Her family moves to the country. He goes off to military school.
At sixteen, he's back. He buys an old Waco bi-plane,

flies it without a license. When the airport gets some flak for letting
him take off from there, he has to park it in his mother's yard.
A pilot, he marries twice. A daughter and son the second marriage.

When Eastern closes its doors without any announcement,
he moves to Saudi Arabia to keep the money coming in.
Years later, she runs into Bill Shaver from Hamilton Avenue

at a Faulkner Conference in Oxford, Mississippi. He tells her
          hometown news:
Robert is home with a tour bus parked in front of his mother's house.
His arrival would be like Hannibal's army on a march, elephants in front.

She calls. He comes for the conference's final night.
He still has the gimpy-legged, cocky walk of a skinny-ass boy.
After downing three margueritas in five minutes, he eats steak,

throws up in the john before the farewell banquet ends.
She has paid for the drinks and the steak. It is his way of keeping
a woman from buying him dinner. The gills of a gentleman.

He sleeps through the evening speaker, wakes up to say he's heard it before.
She's furious, having waited all week to watch this genius of a woman
snatch Faulkner back into glory, out of the hands of academic
          hanging-judges.

They sleep in her Holiday Inn bed, in their clothes like children.
He calls her late one Sunday night, slurry drunk. His daughter needs $3,000
worth of braces. Why is someone in Earle, Arkansas, drinking in his office,

a trailer in back of his mother's house on respectable Hamilton Avenue,
calling someone sitting in a cramped apartment in Bakersfield, California?
What is she supposed to say to a man who has heard it all before?

Approaching sixty, she is out of things to offer. A Hester Prynne,
people call her when things go badly, never if they're going well.
The airline compound in Saudi had a cozy social life. When Robert

was forced into early retirement because of growing deafness, his wife
had already lined up a younger pilot. Hiring herself a whole stable
       of Detroit
lawyers, she and the children stayed in Saudi with a new husband
       and daddy.

Robert was put out to pasture, hobbled for whenever she might need him.
He says he misses his children. "Then, get custody," she says.
He explains his ex-wife is a good mother. "How can a pathological

liar be a *good* mother?" she asks. He's deaf to this scorn so she screams,
"Why have you called *me*? *You picked her.* I was never
paid a penny of child support. I hate this woman!" He needs

a pathological truth-monger about as much as he needed the liar he had.
But she may be as close as he has ever come to a sister.
He's stubborn, was born that way. She's reckless, always has been.

Stubborn and reckless, they have gone through more than a hundred years
between them. Mixed up with the stars is their mongrel faith:
The blinking lights planes carry with them through the dark.

The first touching down of wheels on the runway.
Hannibal taking his elephants through the Alps.
The level earth. Carthage. The lap of the pietà.

Aria from This Opera Called My Life

The one month when friends write to each other in this country...
Hey! Bet you don't know how much we love you.
We'll be better correspondents in the next life!

I'm good about writing back. *The next life? How cavalier.*
How will you ever recognize me?
I'll know you by the pen in your hand.
It was an unlikely stroke of luck that we ran into each other this *lifetime.*
May no Herods blight your holidays
although an unplanned trip into Egypt doesn't sound all that bad right now.

I've pulled all-nighters for a month trying to clear out the cards.
Wiser this year, I saved the envelopes
which make the address book unnecessary.

The ex-relative who engineered my son's marriage to a good Catholic girl
calls on Christmas from New Jersey.
We read two of your poems at dinner tonight.
I can tell how clever she thinks herself for working me in
without having to include me.

I laugh as if charmed. *Don't do this to me.*
Then I sober up. *Did my poems enjoy themselves?*
Did they eat well? How nice of you to invite them.

My son has called from Madrid and left a message.
It's Christmas Eve here. We're about to sit down
with Cristina's family to a Cordon Bleu meal compliments of Juan.
I know you're gone.
I want this message to be there when you get home.

Another ex-relative writes. *You're a wonderful woman*
and I'm grateful for the ways you've touched my life in the past year.
Marilyn calls to tell me Charlotte has been killed by a train.
I tell her about *wonderful woman.*
In her everyday wisdom, Marilyn says, *Yes,*
that means you haven't been any bother to them.
Another card arrives. *You're an Angel.*
Still up all night, still answering every cap pistol shot my way...
I'm a hag. The only man known to call me Princess
is also the only man known to call me Cunt.
A football player who once hailed me as Blondie
yelled Bitch *at me two minutes later*
from a safe twenty feet away. Watching me turn,
he suddenly understood the swishy long hair was only a metaphor.
In a loud whine, he said, 'I was just trying to be friendly.'
His doing that meant I needn't get the snot beaten out of me
while I tried to slug him.
I said, 'It doesn't work with strangers, does it?
Save friendly *for people whose names you know.'*
I don't want even to guess the flip side of Angel
but the shadow of hag *doesn't scare me.*

My son sends a jewelry box handmade in Portugal.
Proof the country has trade schools for the mentally retarded.
They're given plywood stained mahogany to work with.
Doing better woodcraft himself in sixth grade,
he made a bookstand for me. I own books but no jewelry.
His wife helps make these decisions now.

A friend also sends me a box,
a much more expensive box but just as useless.
It's from a handcraft galleria in Montrose.
This is like giving bric-a-brac to a street person as if that will improve
　　　his life.

I live in an apartment, one month away from homeless.
The second month I don't work I'll be there.

My mother died with a houseful of cheap trinkets
given to her by people she had helped.
My mother died the loneliest woman in the world.
In a cluttered house.
She honored the lopsided world by keeping its token gifts.

My heart was stabbed ages ago but the cavalier
gestures of Christmas twist the knife.
Wanting to see my granddaughter with her parents,
I asked my son to send a photograph of the three of them.
It's been months now. I know that I'll never get it.

The only matching earrings I own were a gift from my son.
They are the last he gave me: Toledo steel and gold.
But I still have the single earrings of those given when
he was young. They improvise together as pairs.
I would never throw away the only family jewels.

An architect could draw me blueprints for a house.
As talented as he is, it would be a marvel of a house
if he put his heart into it.
That the house would never be built is beside the point.
I am making my son's daughter a book about willow leaves.
I sent her a car so that he could re-live his sweaty hot-wheels childhood.
People who know you can give you things no one else can.

The Christmas conversation with New Jersey was preceded by a gift.
My polite thank-you note probably prompted the call.
The gift was a cosmetic bag with a bar of lavender soap inside.
I don't wear cosmetics. I haven't seen a *bar* of soap since 1970
and have been celebrating the disappearance of that mess ever since.

Because she's a reader, I send her copies of the best books I read each year.
In return, she's made me a recycling station for the unwanted gifts in her
        house.
Swords are the essential gesture of the cavalier. Gallantry is secondary.
Dagger in hand, MacBeth stands over the sleeping Duncan, his kinsman.

The only thing I've liked was the card from my Uncle Erwin,
a man who stands six-six without any boots.
He wrote, *Hello, little darlin.*
Come to see us when you can.
I'd already sent him a card.
Send me your blessing. And word that you are there.

The only other thing I have to say is for
the loneliest woman in the world who is dead now:
        In the next life, may you be a banner —
        a prayer flag unfurled
        on the highest mountain in Tibet.
        And may I be the wind.

Safari Through the South

I've reeked of resistance every day of my life.
Even the planes I fly on arrive late.
Shish, with plans, stands at the gate. Because it's cold in the Garden
        of Gethsemane
after midnight and even liquor stores close, we find a Holiday Inn
near the airport. Morning gets in our faces and demands a long day.
        We enter
the rarified air of the Grand Hotel at Point Clear to meet up with Vandy
        and her girls.
Then it's Pensacola again to pick up my son and pregnant daughter-in-law
for three days on the Redneck Riviera near Perdido Key.
Side-saddling into Pensacola one last time, Shish, Vandy, her three daughters,
and I – the whole congregation, so to speak – improvise a makeshift goodbye
as my son and Cristina disappear for another year
between icicle teeth into the jowls of Berlin.

Birmingham is a miracle of steering wheels, cruise controls and sunset.
We stay overnight at the Crown Sterling Suites, aswarm
with businessmen so sterling in their suits that I cannot tell
which are after crowns and which simply want the sweets.
A quick visit to Vandy's in-laws proves Peggy Guggenheim could have
lived in the suburbs and never been noticed. Leaving Vandy
amid the debris of a half-remodeled house, Shish and I proceed to Bobbye's.
Dalton's country club got mentioned in some drugstore novel.
Bobbye insists that's reason enough to eat crab crepes there.
We spend the afternoon hunting T. Blair in Ocoee and visiting
the Benton cemetery so that I can see John Paul's military plaque
which Bobbye spent $300 to mount after Aunt Phyliss's nagging her to death.
Everyone knows John Paul detested the Army,
especially the hours and months and years he was in it.

Propped on stilts with the hill falling away below, Bobbye's deck runs
the length of her house. An old-fashioned wooden swing made in
Perfect, Georgia, holds me out there. The deck is larger than T. Blair's house.
He's been through so much whiskey and so many wives – wives who
spent his money and held onto all his mama's curly maple sideboards
and gargoyled brass lamps – it takes Bobbye, Shish and me three hours
to locate his cabin. We just keep trying dirt roads until we get the right one.
Even so, the doctors have him on prozac *and* valium.
Sleeping until eleven each morning, I find Shish's afternoon naps
totally unwarranted. But she persists in them everywhere we go.
I pass the time gazing into space. The screened verandah with
ceiling fans at the beach, air conditioner panting itself to death inside.
Bobbye's deck at night with katydids incessant in their calls back and forth,
loud enough to shatter nerves and let one know, once and for all,
that insects have no interest in solitude.
With brains smaller than the eye can see, they ride the swirl
of their own noise and get along quite well, mating themselves
into looking like pale green leaves. A million of them are in Bobbye's
trees and her backyard isn't that big. Smarter than hell
and the Catholic Church doesn't have anything on them
when it comes to propagating the race, in spite of
those doctrines piled up to heaven on mahogany desks.

After Bobbye's, it's Dee's house in Knoxville and Gary's backyard.
Dogs wherever we go. Baxter down at the beach. Nikki in Dalton.
Puffer and Rascal at T. Blair's. Puffer because he puffs the whole way
whenever T. Blair makes him go for a walk. Rascal is Chow.
Chows have purple tongues, come from Tibet.
Dog introductions include these details
to offset the mongrel tendencies rampant in the South.
Family traits are a big deal, the only world history you're
required to master. An obsession with tongues
will show up every time.
Dee's Irish. Her dog Guinness surreptitiously pees

on the carpet. Shish's dog, Tyke, is waiting for us in Lexington.
There's no dog at Gary's. Gary sits in his own backyard
under the trees without deck or verandah. He's not
the man to put up with dogshit.

We don't get to see Fenner. He's gone. As a weekend destination,
Brooklyn sounds more desperate than heroic.
Our visit would have done him good.
Already overloaded with females, we don't call his wife.
She shows her garterbelt to senior partners. Even though
Reba doesn't exactly like her, I get Reba to agree more lawyers
should hoochie-koochie. It's preferable to the strut.
Ten-Horse's house is temporarily closed to everyone but him.
He's painting the outside of it nine different shades of camouflage green.
A ten-foot, wrought-iron, Jesus cross leans against one of the frontyard elms.
Large pieces of driftwood hoisted on chains dangle from a child's swingset.
People stop. He tells them nothing's for sale.
The bottle tree gives no shade to the three lawnmowers set out to graze.
Reba refuses to go over. Says he is crazy.
Ten-Horse's eyes tell me he's as much at home in there as he ever was.
It's just that Rabelais, Willie Loman, his buddies have died.

Being married to anyone who enjoys working for the IRS is hard.
Adaptable, Reba managed a son and daughter
out of one before impounding his house and car.
And she still talks to Seeper whenever he shows signs of being human.
His mother needs care. Seeper's sisters are leaving it
entirely in his hands. For a man who has never even tried to imagine
helping someone, a sudden change of direction like that is
overwhelming. He hasn't the foggiest notion how to begin.
Good men seldom move women the way an s.o.b. does
when his tight heart tries two or three thumps as experiment.
Terrified to learn exactly what feelings are, Seeper's smart.
No adult with half a mind would willingly agree to give

himself over to love. It's just most of us can't
help ourselves. We got started long before we had any sense.

Turnip greens, pork barbecues, green beans cooked in vinegar,
tomatoes, olive oil and garlic, cole slaw shredded so fine
there's nothing left to chew except the coolness of its taste,
petite filet mignons so thick, so red-meat solid, so big I can feel
the heart attack in my future as vividly as I could when I ate
clotted cream in St. Ives. And always hushpuppies
with anything pulled out of the water.

Flipped out of a teaspoon into vats of screaming hot grease,
not those lumpy, dry things that taste dead.
Hushpuppies vary in integrity about as much as Yorkshire pudding does.
A million bad things can be had in this world.
They all go by the names of the good things.

From Knoxville, it's straight to Lexington. After all the sashaying around,
I'm not prepared. When I insist on hot tea, Shish wants to use
the drive-through at McDonald's. *What I really need
is to sit down for a minute on something that isn't moving,*
I say through clenched teeth. I'm no more than an arrow
flying toward an apple. Giving away my little pile of free will
to a machine that's pretending it's the Beat Generation on the road
is as bad as helping out one of the foolish virgins.
The South scares me. It's so easy to do nothing here.
But the summer heat works like a Church dispensation.
When I moved from Wyoming to California years ago,
a woman asked me why I was doing it. I told her,
I want to sweat again. I've forgotten what it feels like.

Penita gave me a Virgin of Guadalupe lighter for the cigarettes constantly
in my hand at my son's wedding last summer. As Shish and I drive by
a DON'T LET THE DEVIL GET YOU billboard, rooted in the hillside

along this freeway that runs like a silver ribbon through the lush green
of Appalachia, I try to imagine a Southern Baptist cigarette lighter.
The demure figure of the Virgin with her hands folded in prayer replaced
by a replica of Falwell shaking his finger at me, exactly
the kind of big-time sinner he would like to get his hands on.
I imagine him in the depths of my messy purse.

I cannot take in all that rushes past me. Yet little of it has changed.
This woman with such abundant green, unkempt hair
never shows her face but puts her hand up occasionally to touch the ribbon,
to see if it is still in place. Somewhere in West Virginia at the top of her head,
the ribbon is tied in a bow. When Shish gets home, she'll play with Tyke,
fix a Scotch and water before sitting in her Morris chair, twisting
her legs into the lotus position. She'll read the newspapers,
call friends on the phone. This catching up, like folding a napkin after
dinner, places her back inside her life.

Tonight we'll talk. Shish's blue eyes, my green ones will look
without compassion, without ill-will into the other's.
The sameness of grits and red-eye gravy is in us.
Having known each other since seventeen, our children grown,
we have thirty fallow years as distance between us.
They speak of chosen loyalties, inevitable betrayals.

Yet we are green as the rained-on leaves outside.
Our voices, going nowhere in particular, will grope their way
downward through the dark earth of all that's never said.
Leaves are willful creatures and live their lives tossed by the winds.
Roots lie safe in the ground, know the terms of unconditional surrender.